Moban and Sky's MINDFUL ADVENTURE

written by Bernie Leonard
illustrated by Chris Taylor

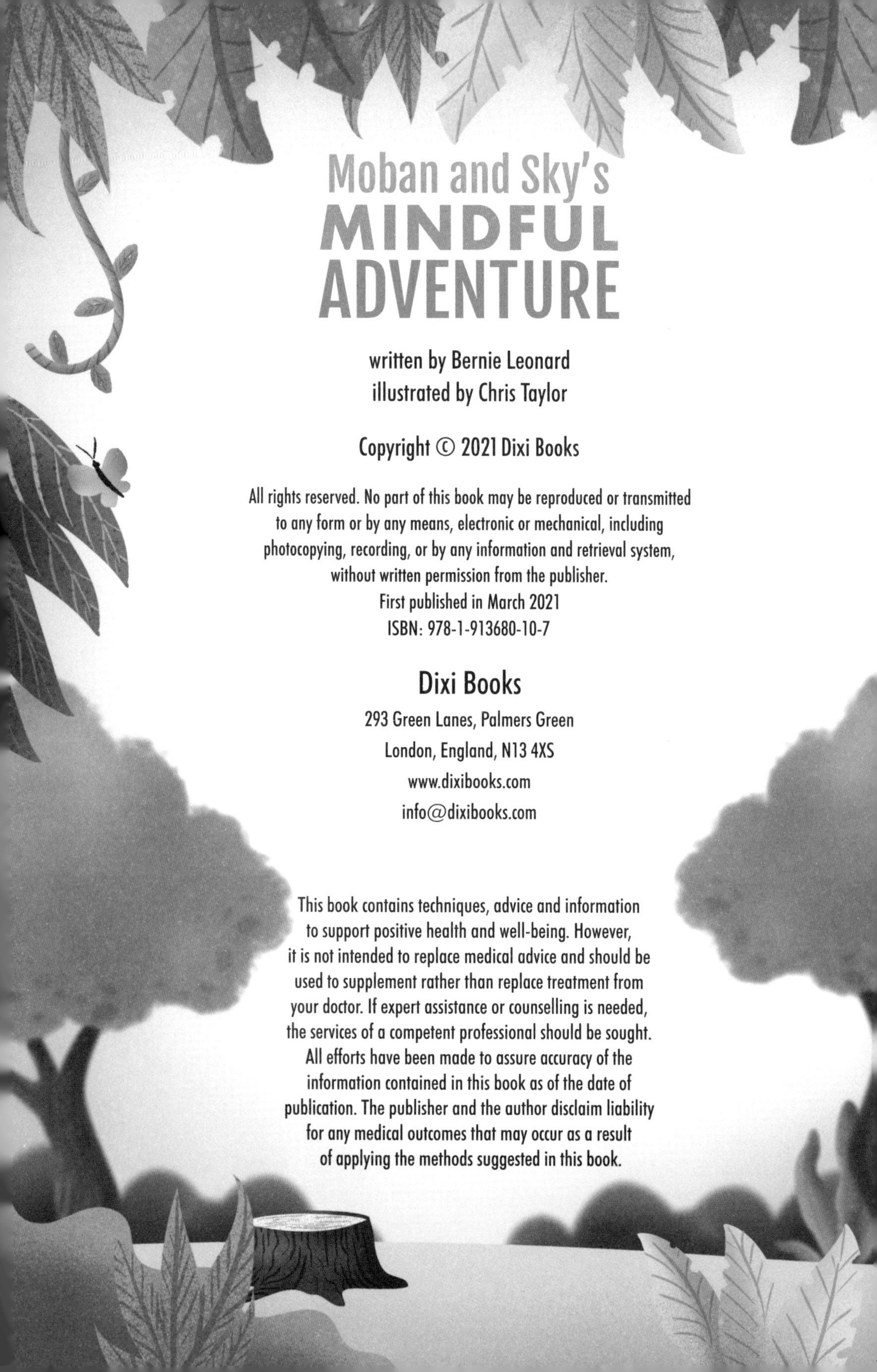

Moban and Sky's MINDFUL ADVENTURE

written by Bernie Leonard
illustrated by Chris Taylor

First published in March 2021
ISBN: 978-1-913680-10-7

Dixi Books
293 Green Lanes, Palmers Green
London, England, N13 4XS
www.dixibooks.com
info@dixibooks.com

CONTENTS

Track the impact of your very own mindfulness journey over the next six weeks. Take our simple stress and mindfulness tests today and in six-weeks time visit:
www.mindfulme-hw.co.uk/primary-pshe/

AUDIENCE

This book in the first instance is geared towards children with the support of their parents/carers/teachers. The intention of this book is to improve the health and well-being of people of all ages, by equipping them with the well-being tools to live a healthier and happier life.

A NOTE ABOUT THE AUTHOR

Bernie Leonard lives in West Yorkshire, England with her two amazing children Beth and Ben, and her soulmate Simon. She is a psychology graduate and a qualified teacher of Mindfulness. After teaching Psychology successfully over two decades, she re-trained as a Mindfulness teacher and now runs her own well-being business, Mindful Me Health & Well-Being Ltd. www.mindfulme-hw.co.uk

A NOTE ABOUT MINDFULNESS

It can be easy to rush through life without fully appreciating what it has to offer. Many of us are not living our best life, because we are preoccupied with the past and the future. We can live our lives on autopilot, in an almost mechanical state, functioning without really thinking. When we live in the past it can be depressing, when we are fixated on the future it can sometimes cause anxiety. The present is the only time we can live in and that is sacred, so why miss it?

I would define mindfulness as stepping off life's merry-go-round and taking the time to notice, noticing what's happening right now, both internally and externally, without judgement. When we practise mindfulness, we begin to amplify our senses and learn how to direct our attention to the present moment. It's almost like seeing things through the eyes of a child, stopping to smell the roses and making time to listen to the birds sing.

If we spend all our waking hours glued to our phones, social media and devices we may miss the beauty right in front of us.

Mindfulness helps develop our understanding of how our brain works, increases our concentration, our sense of calm and our compassion for ourselves and others. As a result, developing our practice makes us happier, healthier, and more skilful at responding to difficult emotions; overall, it increases our focus and enhances our performance.
WE FEEL CONNECTED!

The practice is over two and a half thousand years old and originated from Buddhist philosophy and tradition. That said, you don't need to be of any religious denomination to practise mindfulness. The ability to develop mindfulness skills can be cultivated by anyone.

In the following pages, we will share with you seven mindfulness techniques that, with daily practice, will have a profound positive effect on your well-being and the young people in your care. The guidance is to practise each one of the techniques for a week over a period of six weeks and record what you notice (the investigation bit!). Follow the advice on the contents page, which gives you a suggested order in which to practise the different strategies. You will also find a weekly template for investigation at the back of this book, which you can duplicate and adapt to record what you notice after each practice for that week.

To maximise the benefits, at the end of the six weeks, make a plan of how you are going to integrate all the practices into your daily life, using the example at the back of the book as your guide.

MEET SKY AND MOBAN

Meet Sky, she's so stressed, has lost all her confidence, and she can no longer do her job – nothing's working as it should be.

Sky can't eat, she can't sleep, she feels dreadful and she is in a constant state of anxiety and fear. Her beautiful protective fur is even starting to fall out.

She can no longer eat honeybees, because now that her fur has thinned out, she's not protected from their stings.

Sky has also lost her powerful all protecting pong and feels she can longer keep safe from predators!

Meet Moban, the Mindful monkey. He's living the life; happy, healthy and carefree.

Sky meets Moban...

Moban asks how he can help her. Sky tells him her story and how she can no longer release her pong.

"How can you help?

"I want to be happy, healthy and carefree like you. I just know my powerful defensive weapon will return then, and I'll be equipped to do my job properly once again."

"You're on, Sky! I'm more than happy to help you develop your superpowers."

LET'S FIND OUT HOW MOBAN CAN HELP SKY STOP WORRYING, BOOST HER CONFIDENCE, FEEL STRONG AND FULL OF ENERGY AGAIN. AND MAYBE THEN, SHE'LL FIND HER PONG.

WEEK 1

MINDFUL EATING: TECHNIQUE 1

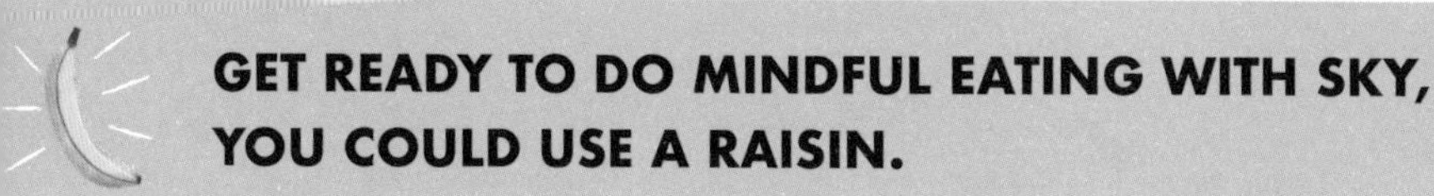

GET READY TO DO MINDFUL EATING WITH SKY, YOU COULD USE A RAISIN.

"Let's start with something easy, try looking at these berries like you've never seen them before."

"Don't be silly, they're just berries."

"You'll need to trust me, just go with it...

1. **Hold them in the palm of your hand, examine them closely. What do they look like?**
2. **Which colours can you see, are they all the same colour?**
3. **Hold them up to the light, do they change colour?**
4. **Are they slimy, smooth or soft, what do they feel like?**
5. **Lift the berries up to your nose, what do they smell like?**
6. **Try putting one on your tongue, now move it around your mouth, what does it feel like?**
7. **And now take a bite, how does it taste?**
8. **Ask yourself, what did I notice?**

"You can do this with just about any activity, it's just a great way of getting you to focus on what's happening right now. How did it make you feel?"

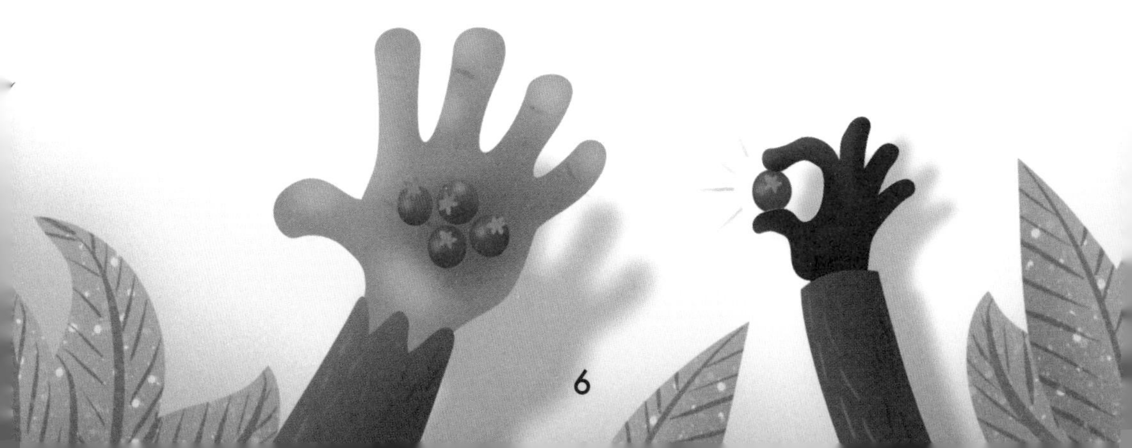

"It made me feel calm, I was just thinking about and enjoying the berries."

"Exactly! And when you really work at concentrating on what's happening right this moment, it helps you stop worrying about the past or getting anxious about what's going to happen next."

"Now try doing this, we call it mindful eating, for three mouthfuls of one meal each day and investigate what you notice. Taking the time to investigate what you notice Sky is so so important!"

"What do you mean by investigation?"

"Just do exactly what we did with the berries, notice the aromas, tastes and textures - get practising!"

Now Sky's started to notice what she's eating, she's actually eating less and enjoying it more, noticing all the wonderful aromas and tastes. It's almost like her excellent sense of smell has been awakened, a power she'd almost forgotten she had amid all the stress, she wasn't even noticing what she was putting in her mouth, nor whether she was hungry or full.

"Note to self – must keep practising Sky!!"

AND WHY DON'T YOU TRY MINDFUL EATING FOR ONE MEAL A DAY FOR THE NEXT WEEK? JUST FOLLOW STEPS 1- 8, FOR 3 MOUTHFULS OF YOUR CHOSEN MEAL - GO ON, GIVE IT A GO AND DON'T FORGET TO RECORD HOW IT MAKES YOU FEEL!

THE GROUNDING TECHNIQUE: TECHNIQUE 2

Next for a practice to improve Sky's confidence.

"Sky, are you up for a little confidence booster?" She nods, "Well follow me."

"Now sit down, placing your feet firmly on the ground, we're just going to spend a few moments focusing on your breathing. Closing your eyes, notice where the air comes into your body, try following it right down into your tummy. Be aware of how your body changes as you breathe in and out. Try placing your hand on your tummy and notice how it moves slightly as you breathe in and out."

YOU CAN DO THIS WITH SKY. SIMPLY SIT UPRIGHT IN YOUR CHAIR WITH BOTH YOUR FEET PLANTED FIRMLY ON THE FLOOR AND YOUR HANDS ON YOUR LAP, CLOSING YOUR EYES – WE'LL CALL THIS YOUR MINDFULNESS POSITION.

"Now continue breathing normally, with both your hands on your knees, imagine you've got a big beam of light and shine it towards your feet.

"Digging your powerful claws into the floor remind yourself that you are connected to the ground. Feel confident knowing the ground is always there to support you...

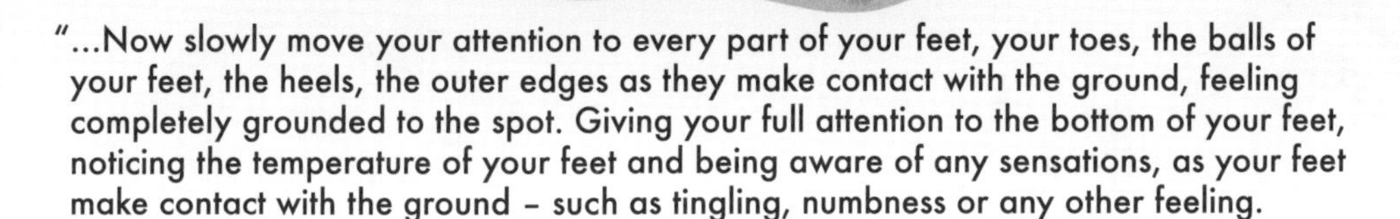

"...Now slowly move your attention to every part of your feet, your toes, the balls of your feet, the heels, the outer edges as they make contact with the ground, feeling completely grounded to the spot. Giving your full attention to the bottom of your feet, noticing the temperature of your feet and being aware of any sensations, as your feet make contact with the ground – such as tingling, numbness or any other feeling.

"Now slowly moving your attention back up your body, from your feet to your ankles, to your knees, to your tummy and on your next breath slowly open your eyes. How did that feel Sky?"

"I felt peaceful and quiet. My mind wasn't busy, because I was just concentrating on my feet, right here, right now."

"Great! When you're putting all your energy into feeling your feet, it's more difficult to focus on everything you're worrying about. Try this next time you need a little extra confidence boost, or you simply need to focus. Keep a note of what happens."

Each day practising her new technique
she feels her confidence starting to rise.

NOW TRY USING THE GROUNDING TECHNIQUE THIS WEEK WHEN YOU WANT TO IMPROVE YOUR FOCUS OR WHEN YOU FEEL YOU WANT TO HELP YOURSELF BE A BIT STRONGER OR MORE CONFIDENT.
YOU CAN DO THIS TECHNIQUE WITH YOUR EYES OPEN OR CLOSED, JUST REMEMBER, WHEN YOU'VE FINISHED THE PRACTICE DON'T FORGET TO INVESTIGATE HOW IT MADE YOU FEEL.

THE SCIENCE BIT PART 1

"Moban, I'm ready for number 3."

"Before I teach you the next practice, we need to have a little biology lesson because once you develop your superpowers, I don't want you to lose them ever again.

"Did you know that stress can have all these effects on your body, aching joints, headaches, spots, tummy aches and just simply feeling unwell?

"The fight-or-flight response is both normal and helps protect us, it evolved over hundreds of millions of years to enable our ancestors to protect themselves from predators and stay alive."

SOME STRESS CAN IN FACT BE A GOOD THING FOR YOU; IT CAN GIVE YOU AN EXTRA BURST OF ENERGY WHEN PLAYING COMPETITIVE SPORTS, DURING EXAMS OR HAVING TO SPEAK IN PUBLIC. HOWEVER, WHEN THE PRIMITIVE FIGHT-OR-FLIGHT RESPONSE IS ACTIVATED TOO OFTEN OR FOR TOO LONG IT CAN HAVE A DETRIMENTAL EFFECT ON YOUR BODY AND YOUR BRAIN.

"Wait a minute Moban, slow down. What's the fight-or-flight response?"

"Our bodies are really smart; the fight-or-flight response is our body's automatic response to something we see as a threat. When we see danger, an alarm bell goes off in our brain, adrenaline floods into our body activating our nervous system, our heart pumps faster to increase the flow of blood to our muscles, we breathe faster to take in oxygen, we start to sweat to keep our bodies cool – we are at our strongest to fight or run away.

"When the danger has passed, the part of our nervous system responsible for calming us down (it's called the PNS – Parasympathetic Nervous System) kicks in, our heart rate slows down, and we start to breathe normally. When someone is suffering from continuous stress for a long time, the PNS is not activated as regularly as it should be and the person can be in a constant state of anxiety, which can be really damaging to our health."

NOW IT'S TIME FOR YOU TO BE THE SCIENTIST AND DO YOUR OWN RESEARCH – YOU COULD RESEARCH HOW STRESS IMPACTS ON YOUR BODY AND MIND, AND THE BENEFITS OF PRACTISING MINDFULNESS.

YOU COULD CREATE A DISPLAY TO SHOWCASE THE FINDINGS OF YOUR RESEARCH.

"Moban, can you tell me a little more about how the brain responds to stress and how practising my new strategies can help?"

"There are lots of parts of the brain that are involved in our response to stress. One of the most important of those is the amygdala, which is, the area of the brain responsible for the perception of emotions, anger, fear, sadness, as well as the controlling of aggression. When this area of the brain detects that we see something as a threat, it sets off the alarm which triggers the fight-or-flight response. Another part of the brain that can be affected by stress is the hippocampus. The job of this part of the brain is to store and recall memories, it's also really important for learning. But when the amygdala is constantly activated, it can't do its job properly and we can forget things and find it difficult to learn new information. The pre-frontal cortex (PFC) is the part of the brain that's in charge of decision making and concentration. Continuous stress causes shrinking of the PFC, which results in us finding it hard to make wise decisions and that's why when we're stressed, we can sometimes make bad choices.

"It's not all doom and gloom though, practising Mindfulness can kick start your PNS, decrease your stress and help you have a healthier brain. This in turn can improve your memory and your ability to make wise decisions. By practising your new techniques daily, you can start to calm yourself down, shrink your amygdala and grow your hippocampus and your PFC."

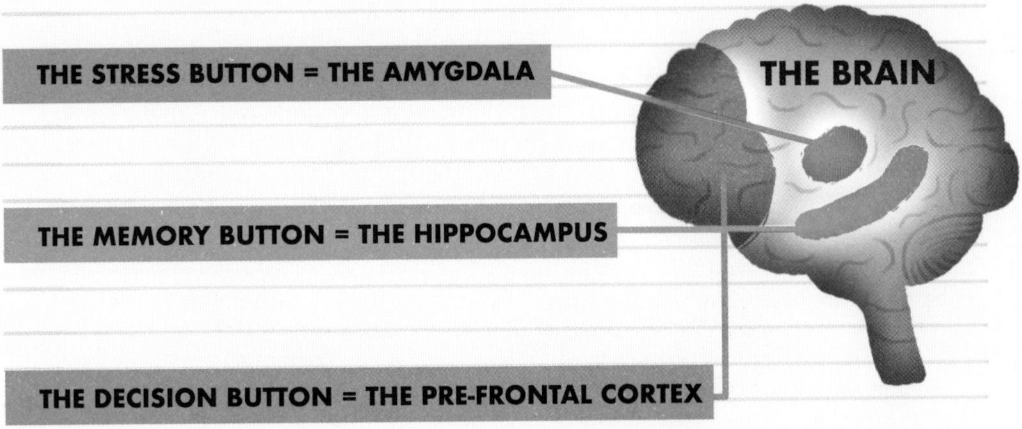

THE BRAIN

THE STRESS BUTTON = THE AMYGDALA

THE MEMORY BUTTON = THE HIPPOCAMPUS

THE DECISION BUTTON = THE PRE-FRONTAL CORTEX

WEEK 2

THE 3 STEP BREATHING SPACE: TECHNIQUE 3

"Wow Moban, now I know how important it is to stay calm and in control. I'm definitely ready for practice 3."

"Here's technique 3, which with practice is going to help your brain look more like mine. Let's start by sitting in your mindfulness position, with your eyes closed...

TAKE A MOMENT TO CONSIDER EACH QUESTION IN STEP 1. DON'T SHOUT OUT YOUR ANSWER, JUST REALLY TRY AND CONCENTRATE ON WHAT YOU CAN NOTICE AS WE SLOWLY GO THROUGH THE QUESTIONS.

STEP1

Just focus on what's happening right now.

What are you thinking right now?

What are you feeling right now, calm, stressed, neutral?

Are you aware of any sensations in your body right now, do you feel any tightness anywhere?

Now try thinking of all three together, thoughts, feelings and body sensations, being aware of what's here right now.

STEP 2

"Switching your attention to your breathing. We are just going to spend a few moments focusing on your breathing. Being aware of where the air comes into your body through your nostrils and try following it right down into your tummy. Notice how your body changes as you breathe in and out. You could try placing your hand on your tummy and notice how it moves slightly as you breathe in and out. Just simply focus on the breath as you inhale and exhale.

STEP 3

"Now moving your hands back to your lap, expand your attention to the whole of your body. Slowly moving your attention from the top of your head, down to your shoulders, down your arms, your fingers. Down your body to your lower back, to your legs and right down to your toes. Then try expanding it a little further to the area around your body. On your next breath slowly open your eyes.

"How did that make you feel Sky?"

"Wow, it made me feel sensational, it gave me the chance to reset and recharge. I feel ready for anything!"

"Well, let's see how your body is looking...

"...Now Sky try doing this twice a day for the next week and don't forget your investigation!"

AND YOU CAN DO THE SAME. PRACTISE THE 3-STEP BREATHING SPACE TWICE A DAY FOR THE NEXT WEEK AND RECORD WHAT YOU NOTICE!

WEEK 3

THE TEN FINGERS OF GRATITUDE: TECHNIQUE 4

"What I've noticed about you Moban is that you're always so positive and you don't seem to worry about anything. What can you do to help me with this Moban?"

"Well, first of all Sky did you know if you spend all your time worrying you get better at worrying and in fact most of the things you actually worry about never actually happen?

"Do you get what I mean Sky?

"This brings me to our next practice, the ten fingers of gratitude, you may find this will help. Appreciating the small things in life can really help you to see things in a more positive way.

"Each night before you go to sleep, or day in your case Sky (skunks are nocturnal you see, they stay awake during the night and sleep during the day) take a moment and look down at your ten fingers and think of ten things you are grateful for that day or night. It doesn't need to be anything major; it could be simply being grateful for the beautiful berries you ate for lunch, the feeling of joy when you realised your fur was starting to grow back.

"Do you know the most happy and successful beings practise gratitude Sky?"

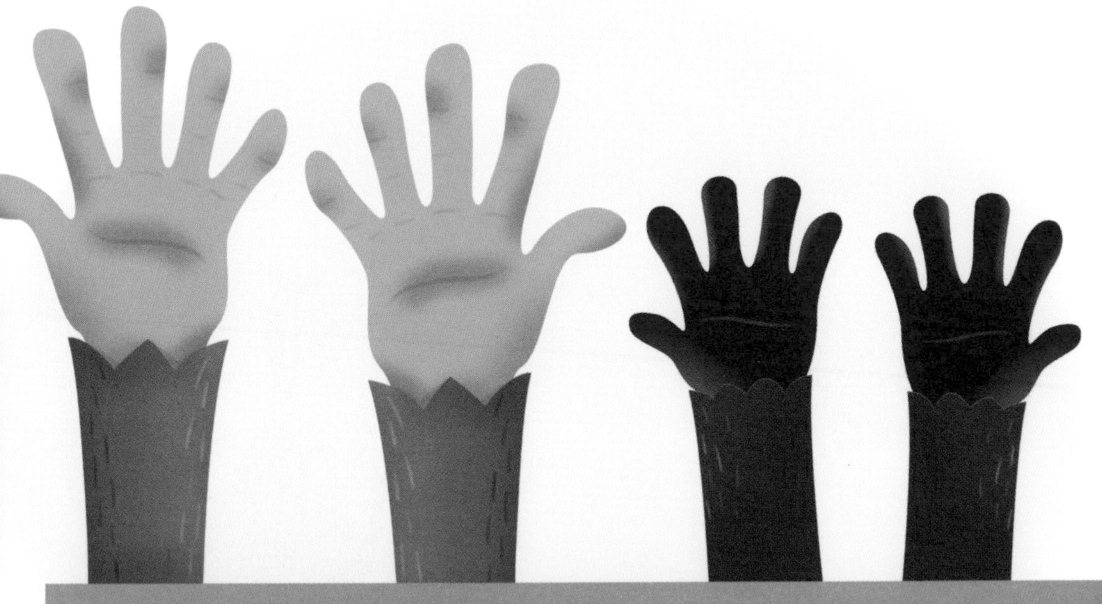

WHY DON'T YOU HAVE A GO, TRY IT TONIGHT BEFORE YOU GO TO SLEEP. WOULDN'T YOU LIKE TO BE HAPPY AND SUCCESSFUL TOO?

THIS IS YOUR PRACTICE FOR THIS WEEK, PRACTISE IT ONCE A DAY AND DON'T FORGET YOUR INVESTIGATION!

WE SUGGEST YOU TRY THE PRACTICE NOW AND HAVE A CLASS DISCUSSION AROUND WHAT YOU COULD INCLUDE IN YOUR GRATITUDE PRACTICE, YOU COULD ALWAYS START WITH FIVE FINGERS AND BUILD UP TO TEN.

THE BODY SCAN: TECHNIQUE 5

"Moban, something I've been trying not to worry about, or shall we say I've been thinking about, how am I going to make time to practise all my new techniques in my busy life?"

"That's a great question Sky, but the simple answer is that you need to slow down to speed up. If you invest in yourself by taking the time to practise your new techniques, you'll start to reap the rewards. As you start being able to control your emotions better, you'll find your anxiety levels will drop, which means you'll find it easier to concentrate, you'll be able to take in new information and you'll be able to remember it when you need it. You'll be able to do things quicker and make fewer mistakes, you won't be wasting your time being distracted and worrying about the same thing over and over again, which will free up time.

"You're going to love our next practice Sky, it's called the Body Scan. The aim of this technique is for you to be aware of the different parts of your body, it helps train your attention and release feelings of frustration and anger. That said, a wonderful side-effect of this technique is, it can help relax your muscles and if you practise it when you go to bed, it helps you get a great night's sleep. If you are someone who wakes up during the night worrying, just snuggle back down and do it again."

YOU CAN DO THIS ONE LAID DOWN ON THE FLOOR LIKE SKY OR SITTING UPRIGHT IN YOUR CHAIR WITH BOTH YOUR FEET PLANTED FIRMLY ON THE FLOOR AND YOUR HANDS ON YOUR LAP, CLOSING YOUR EYES. WHEN YOU'VE FINISHED THE PRACTICE (OR THE NEXT MORNING) DON'T FORGET TO INVESTIGATE HOW IT MADE YOU FEEL.

"Now once you're all settled down in your burrow Sky, lay down on your back, with your arms by your side, in the sleeping position, close your eyes and focus on your breathing.

"Put your hand on your tummy – be aware of your breath moving your tummy up and down. Then when you're ready, with both your arms by your side, imagine you're directing a big beam of light and you're going to use it to scan the whole of your body to bring attention to any sensations that are there. At first you might not feel anything, that's fine. We'll call that neutral.

"We'll start by bringing your attention to your toes, noticing if you feel any tingling in your toes. As you breathe out, move your attention from your toes to the balls of your feet, noticing whether you feel any throbbing in the balls of your feet. Now, let your awareness move to your ankles and on your next outbreath, switch your attention to the calves of your legs and your shins. When you're ready, moving your awareness to your knees, then moving from your knees to your thighs, the whole of your thighs, the front, the back and the sides. Noticing any sensations that are there.

"If your mind wanders, that's fine. No one can pay attention all the time. Just be aware of where your mind goes and then gently bring it back to the area of your body you're working on, that's you working your mindful muscle (each time your mind wanders, bring it back).

THE BODY SCAN: TECHNIQUE 5 (continued)

"When you're ready, move your awareness gently up through the rest of your body to your lower back, slowly move from your lower back to your chest and then your shoulders. Notice any sensations or any tightness as you gently move through your body and if you notice any tightness as you breathe out, release any tension you might have as you exhale.

"Now moving from your shoulders and the base of your neck slowly down to your arms to your fingers, noticing any sensations, any tingling in your fingers. Then slowly moving back up your arms to your neck, then your face and your head, noticing any sensations that are there.

"Finally, spend a few moments paying attention to your whole body and see what you notice, before taking a big stretch and slowly opening your eyes."

WHY DON'T YOU GIVE THIS A GO TONIGHT? YOU CAN TRY IT WHEN YOU'RE LAID DOWN IN YOUR BED LIKE SKY. IT NOT ONLY HELPS YOU SLEEP, BUT IT ALSO HELPS YOU CONCENTRATE IN CLASS, BECAUSE WITH PRACTICE, YOU GET REALLY GOOD AT BRINGING YOUR ATTENTION BACK WHEN YOUR MIND WANDERS OFF.

"Well then how was it, Sky?"

"Moban, you are so clever! How did you know? I was fast asleep before I'd even finished it. I had the best sleep and I woke up feeling better than ever, refreshed and ready to get back out there!"

YOU MIGHT LIKE TO PRACTISE THE BODY SCAN EVERY NIGHT THIS WEEK MAKING A NOTE OF HOW IT MAKES YOU FEEL.

THE SCIENCE BIT PART 2

"Well, before you go on your next foraging mission, I've got another practice to teach you. This is a good one to do at the beginning of your day, or in your case, Sky, at the beginning of your night.

"This is also going to help the part of your brain responsible for keeping your memory on point, because it settles your mind and keeps you calm.

"Scientific studies show that if you do the Sitting Practice (our next practice) for a short time each day, it helps you to pay attention to detail, be more productive and concentrate for longer. It works a little like a snow globe."

"Moban, where are you going with this?"

"Go with it, Sky. If your mind is busy thinking about the past and worrying about the future, think of it like a snow globe in the midst of all that shaking. When you do a practice, your mind gets a chance to settle, just like the snow when you stop shaking the globe.

"When your mind is settled, this helps your hippocampus (the part of your brain responsible for your memory) and your pre-frontal cortex (the part of your brain responsible for making wise decisions) work more effectively because when you remain calm even in challenging times, you stop your amygdala from taking over."

"Just like you told me in our biology lesson, shortly after we met!"

"Yes! Sky, you've got it!"

"How do you know this, Moban?"

"Well Sky, some very clever people at Oxford University in England and probably at lots of other universities too, have taken special pictures of people's brains before and six to eight weeks after practising mindfulness techniques regularly, including some of the ones we've been practising over the past weeks, and they've found these amazing changes."

BEFORE PRACTISING MINDFULNESS

WHAT'S GOING ON IN THE STRESSED BRAIN...

- Enlarged amygdala
- Shrunk hippocampus
- Reduced PFC

AFTER PRACTISING MINDFULNESS

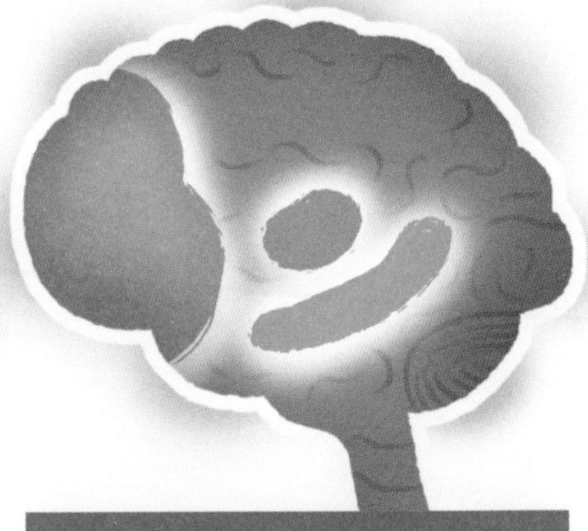

WHAT'S GOING ON IN THE CALM BRAIN...

- Shrunken amygdala
- Enlarged hippocampus
- Enlarged PFC

TO HELP YOU REMEMBER THE SCIENCE BIT, YOU COULD TRY MAKING TWO MODELS OF THE BRAIN, ONE BEFORE PRACTISING MINDFULNESS (SKY'S) AND ONE AFTER (MOBAN'S). IN YOUR MODELS BE SURE TO INCLUDE ALL THE KEY AREAS AFFECTED BY STRESS AND MINDFULNESS.

THE SITTING PRACTICE: TECHNIQUE 6

YOU CAN DO THIS WITH SKY. SIMPLY SIT UPRIGHT IN YOUR CHAIR WITH BOTH YOUR FEET PLANTED FIRMLY ON THE FLOOR AND YOUR HANDS ON YOUR LAP, CLOSING YOUR EYES.

"Are you sitting in your mindfulness position, Sky?

"Let's take a sneak peek inside your mind...

"Now first, bring your attention to sounds, noticing what you can hear right now, internal sounds, such as breathing, external sounds from your environment. Just sitting here, listening to sounds.

"Then when you're ready, moving to focus on your breathing. See if it's possible to follow your breath right down to your tummy, being aware of the sensations of your tummy as the breath moves this area of the body gently in and out.

"Now expand your awareness from your breath to the whole of your body and the area around your body.

"Then when you're ready, moving your attention to your thoughts. Imagine yourself sitting in a movie theatre looking at the screen and seeing your thoughts appear on the screen, staying there for a while and then moving off the screen.

"You might want to label your thoughts useful and not useful.

"If you feel you've left the sitting position and joined the thoughts on the movie screen, just notice this has happened and return to sitting.

"See if it's possible to remain aware of what thoughts are coming up, letting them come and go, like clouds crossing the sky and letting them disperse in their own time.

"Finish by slowly bringing your awareness back to your breathing, feeling your feet on the floor and your body on the chair, gently open your eyes."

"That felt great Moban! I feel calm and in control, my mind was settled, dare I say, I felt empowered to make wise decisions. Now I know exactly where to go to find food and the best time to go."

"I can almost feel your PFC growing, Sky. You're on the journey sister, you're starting to take control of your emotions, powering up your memory and making positive choices!"

THIS IS ONE OF YOUR PRACTICES FOR THIS WEEK. PRACTISE IT ONCE A DAY AND DON'T FORGET YOUR INVESTIGATION!

THE STOP PRACTICE: TECHNIQUE 7

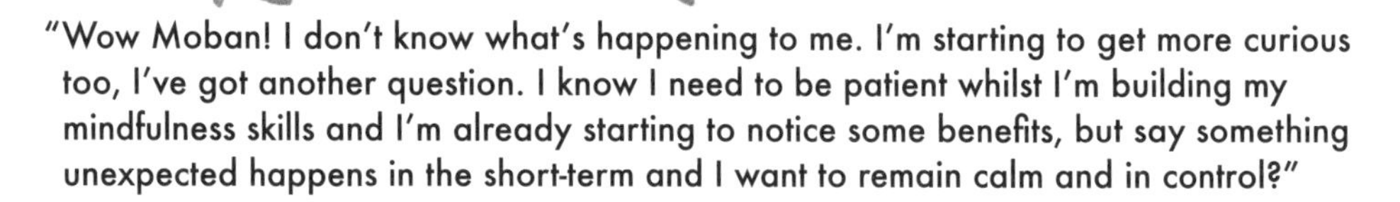

"Wow Moban! I don't know what's happening to me. I'm starting to get more curious too, I've got another question. I know I need to be patient whilst I'm building my mindfulness skills and I'm already starting to notice some benefits, but say something unexpected happens in the short-term and I want to remain calm and in control?"

"Funny you should ask dear friend; I was saving my best little sprinkle of mindful magic until last. It's called the **STOP** practice, quick, but really effective. This little gem can be used to help you calm down and focus, it gives you the space to be able to respond rather than react.

"Do you remember what I said about worrying, Sky?"

"Yes, Moban - most of the things you worry about never actually happen."

"Brilliant, sounds like you've being mindfully listening too. Well, constantly worrying will actually have a detrimental effect on your body and your brain, it will have a harmful effect on your immune system, and you will be more susceptible to illnesses.

"The **STOP** practice can be used to help you settle your mind, calm down and it really helps reduce negative emotions, such as anger or frustration. When you find yourself worrying or getting angry, just STOP!

YOU CAN DO THIS PRACTICE WITH SKY TOO!

S–top whatever you're doing, pause for a moment.

T–ake a conscious breath, simply being aware of yourself breathing. Noticing the movement of your tummy as you breathe in and out. (You may want to take a few conscious breaths if you feel you need to.)

O–bserve your thoughts (and remember to take a moment and consider whether they are thoughts or facts), emotions (just naming your emotions can reduce your fear) and notice your body. (What is your posture saying, are you aware of any sensations, butterflies or tension?)

P–roceed with calmness, clarity and control.

"Now you're ready to respond mindfully to whatever challenges come your way, rather than reacting mindlessly and feeling a little silly."

PLAY AROUND WITH THIS AT FIRST, TRY AND FIT IT INTO YOUR DAY AS OFTEN AS YOU CAN. THEN TRY THIS NEXT TIME A CHALLENGING/UNEXPECTED SITUATION COMES YOUR WAY OR WHEN YOU JUST NEED TO FOCUS. THIS IS YOUR SECOND PRACTICE FOR THIS WEEK, YOU CAN DO THIS TECHNIQUE WITH YOUR EYES OPEN OR CLOSED, JUST DON'T FORGET YOUR INVESTIGATION!

SUMMARY

"Well Sky, my job is complete. I've shared with you the Mindful Magnificent Seven.

"Let's have a quick recap on what they are."

CAN YOU REMEMBER?

"Good luck Sky and..."

Sky buts in, "Yes, I know practise, practise, practise!!"

SIX WEEKS LATER

Six weeks later with daily practice, Sky is living her best life, her coat all shiny and fluffy, her whiskers and eyelashes on point. She's smiling from ear to ear, noticing the beauty of the star-studded jungle sky.

She's sleeping like a baby in her cosy burrow by day and roaming the jungle by night, calm, confident and in control. Conscious of her power – fearing no one.

WITH HER MINDFULNESS TOOLKIT THE SKY'S THE LIMIT!

And yes, Sky's pong is back, 100%!

FINAL NOTE FROM THE AUTHOR

We are always going to face challenges in our lives, no matter how big or small. By equipping ourselves with our mindfulness toolkit we will be in a better place mentally, physically and emotionally to navigate the storms, and live a happier, healthier life.

LIVING A MINDFUL LIFE

A NOTE TO PARENTS, CARERS & TEACHERS

TRY INCORPORATING THE PLAN INTO YOUR DAILY ROUTINE, BEFORE ADAPTING IT FOR YOUR LITTLE DARLINGS.

As Sky's story draws to a close, below are some suggested strategies to support you in living a mindful life, your mindfulness journey has only just begun...

Setting the alarm just two minutes before you need to get up in the morning would give you the time to take a breath and check in with what you're thinking and how you're feeling even before you get out of bed.

Twice a week, you could try incorporating a sitting practice into your mornings, to put you in the best frame of mind to take on the day, especially on those most challenging ones. After your morning practice you'll then be ready to enjoy your shower with full awareness, amplifying all your senses.

If you catch public transport to school/work, you could incorporate a 3 Step Breathing Space into your journey to refresh your neurological processes before you take on the challenges of the day. Even if you drive to work maybe you could leave 3 minutes earlier and enjoy a breathing space before you leave your car.

LIVING A MINDFUL LIFE (continued)

At lunch, be mindful for at least 3 mouthfuls, take the time to enjoy the aromas and the taste of your food.

At your lunch break, how about walking mindfully, feeling the ground through your shoes, taking note of the sounds, sights and smells around you?

Before you re-enter the family home in the afternoon/evening, you could practice a Breathing Space to transform you from the school/work you to the fully attentive daughter/son, mother/father, wife/husband, best friend you.

Anytime throughout the day when a potentially stressful situation arises, you could use STOP (Stop, Take a breath, Observe, Proceed) as a short practice to give you the time to consider your response and take you out of autopilot.

At the end of each day remember your 10 Fingers of Gratitude, you'll start to notice more and more positive things around you.

In bed, you could try doing the Body Scan to help reset and replenish your body and soul. With regular practice, you'll be reaping the rewards of your practice and you'll start to notice the focus of your attention, you'll start to become more productive and efficient in all that you do as a result of training. Don't forget the added bonus that you'll get to sleep more easily and stay asleep.

Next time you're sitting a test, competing in sport, speaking in public or even making a difficult phone call, make time for a 3 Step Breathing Space before you start and keep grounded through your feet throughout. Or if a difficult situation approaches without any warning, stick with the grounding!

Just remember all these small changes will have a massive positive impact on your health and well-being. Good luck, keep going and be more calm, confident and in control.

EVEN A LITTLE CHANGE CAN HAVE A MASSIVE IMPACT

TEMPLATE FOR INVESTIGATION

Adapt the template below to record your weekly practice...

Home Practice Log week 2 - place a tick or a comment in each box.

Day	Using the guidance to start with, before going solo, practise the 3 Step Breathing Space twice a day for the next week.		Comments on the 3 Step Breathing Space What did you notice?	Try the Grounding Technique when you want a little confidence booster or when you just want to focus, recording what you noticed.
Monday				
Tuesday				
Wednesday				
Thursday				
Friday				
Saturday				
Sunday				

ACKNOWLEDGEMENTS

I'd like to thank my wonderful mindfulness teachers and friends, for all their support along the way.

Geraldine Breakwell Mindfulness Practice – who taught me the MBCTL (Mindfulness Based Cognitive Therapy for Life) course as developed by Paul Bernard, Chris Cullen and William Kuyken at The University of Oxford.

To Karen Atkinson MindfulnessUK – who taught me the IMPCC (Integrating Mindfulness & Compassion in Professional Practice) accredited by the Counselling and Psychotherapy Central Awarding Body (CPCAB).

To Angie Ward MindfulnessUK – who taught me Minding Your Health in Education (MYHE).

To Teresa Wort Qualified Mindfulness and Compassion Teacher for her wise words.

Thank you to all the amazing authors, whose works have helped shape my own teaching and now impacted on Moban's guidance.

Mark Williams and Dr Danny Penman 2011. *Mindfulness: A practical guide to finding peace in a frantic world.* Piatkus.

Kristin Neff. 2011. *Self-Compassion.* Harper Collins Publishers

Rick Hanson. 2009. *Buddha's Brain.* New Harbinger Publications. Inc

Ruby Wax. 2016. *A Mindfulness Guide for the Frazzled.* Penguin Life.

Chris Bergstrom. 2017. *Mindfulness and the brain made easy.*

I'd like to give a special thanks to my family and friends for supporting me throughout my very own mindful adventure, without them none of this would have been possible.

**Let us know what you think.
Please share the impact of your journey on our social media accounts.**

- *dixibooks* (Facebook)
- *dixibooks* (Instagram)
- *dixibooks* (Twitter)
- *Mindful Me Health&Well-Being* (Facebook)
- *Mindfulme_HW* (Twitter)

Now it's time to measure the impact of your very own mindfulness adventure. It's time for you to re-take our simple stress and mindfulness tests by visiting
www.mindfulme-hw.co.uk/primary-pshe/